HOW TO SPEAK
ANI
MAL

Copyright © 2022 by Lindy Mattice.

Published by Bushel & Peck Books, a family-run publishing house in Fresno, California, that believes in uplifting children with the highest standards of art, music, literature, and ideas. Find beautiful books for gifted young minds at www.bushelandpeckbooks.com.

Type set in Tomarik, Special Elite, and Josefin Sans
Cover and book design by David Miles

All visuals licensed from Shutterstock.com as follows: Ermolaev Alexander (2); Pixel-Shot (7, 49); Susan Schmitz (8, 10); Emily on Time (9); Megan Betteridge (11); Fotodrobik (12); Eva_Blanco (13, 23); Monika Vosahlova (14); Utekhina Anna (15); Eric Isselee (16, 62, 79, 90, 104, 113); WilleeCole Photography (16, 24, 26); Elayne Massaini (17); Viki2win (18); Jucadima (19); Smit (20-21); Iryna Kalamurza (22); Strelka (25); Gladskikh Tatiana (27); Tomasz Wrzesien (28); Koldunov Alexey (29); Sara Petersson (30); DenisNata (31); Seregraff (31); Koktaro (32); Viktoriia Rusian (33); Kasefoto (34); Okssi (35); Foxhound Photos (36); Photocreo Michal Bednarek (37, 57); Ekaterina Kolomeets (38); Nevodka (39); Dora Zett (40); Smrm1977 (41); Kuttelvaserova Stuchelova (42-43); Oleksandr Lytvynenko (44, 48); Kaewmanee Jiangsihui (45); Prapon Srinakara (46-47); Photomaster (50-51); Jiang Hongyan (52, 56); Nattaro Ohe (53); Litvalifa (54); Grassflowerhead (55); Viktoria Szabo (58); May_Chanikran (60); Olexander Kozak (61); aDam Wildlife (63); Stephan Morris (64); Yalcin Kahya (65); UniqSnaps (66); Vyaseleva Elena (68); Anastasiia Chystokoliana (69); JakPhos (70); Christine Bird (71); DarAnna (72); Tracy Starr (73); Feng Yu (74); Fantom_rd (75); Stock_Shot (77); Nynke van Holten (78); Tsekhmister (80); Olesya Zhuk (81); Natalia7 (82); EniSine (83); Igor Kovalchuk (84); New Africa (85); Elya Vatel (86); Werner Sigg (87); irin-k (88); Chorch (89, 101); Vovan (90); Rita_Kochmarjova (92, 116); Cynoclub (93); Beth Trudeau (94); Victoria Ray (95); Galyna Syngaievska (97); Olena Kurashova (98); Daisy Daisy (99); Kozirsky (100); Photok.dk (101); Vasily Kovalev (102); Lenkadan (103); Bildagentur Zoonar GmbH (105); bmf-foto.de (106); Anna Hudorozkova (107); Willcox (108); Marie Charouzova (109); Makarova Viktoria (110); Perry Correll (111); Arthorse (112); Christian Musat (114); Silviu-Florin Salomia (115); BigBoom (117); PetlinDmitry (118); DedeDian (119); Thawatchai Thandee (120); Kurit Afshen (121); Kamnuan (122); Cherdchai Chaivimol (123); Vaclav Sebek (125); Shark_749 (127); UfaBizPhoto (128); Nynke van Holten (129, 120); Tatyana Vyc (131); Chonlasub Woravichan (132); Andrej Jakubik (133); Andrey Armyagov (135); Buna Una (136); Dmitrii Startcev (137); Waraphorn Aphai (138); Mongkolchon Akesin (139); Aleron Val (141); Visivastudio (142); Grigorev Mikhail (143); patterns by Katyalitvin; pet icons by Davooda, Webicon, Panuwach, ProfiTrollka, and LineTale; graph paper pattern by Inspired-Fiona.

Bushel & Peck Books is dedicated to fighting illiteracy all over the world.
For every book we sell, we donate one to a child in need—book for book. To nominate a school or organization to receive free books, please visit www.bushelandpeckbooks.com.

LCCN: TK   ISBN: 9781638190431

First Edition   Printed in China   10 9 8 7 6 5 4 3

HOW TO SPEAK
ANI MAL

Decode the Secret Language
of Dogs, Cats, Birds,
Reptiles, and More!

LINDY MATTICE

BUSHEL
& PECK
BOOKS

CONTENTS

Introduction / 6

DOGS

The Play Bow / 8
Rolling Over / 10
Eye Contact / 12
Tail Posture / 16
Ear Language / 18

Nose & Lip Licking / 22
Yawning / 23
Leaning / 24
People Licking / 26
Rear End Sniffing / 28

CATS

Tails / 30
Thumping & Flicking of Tail / 32
Eyes / 34
Kneading / 36
Purring / 37

Meowing / 38
Butt Presentation / 39
Licking / 40
Hunting / 42
Belly Up / 44

RABBITS

Loafing / 46
Flopping & Sprawling / 48
Periscoping / 49
Binkying & Zooming / 50
Purring / 52

Alert Posture & Ears / 53
Grooming / 54
Cautious Behavior / 56
Thumping / 58
Circling / 60

BIRDS

Eye Pinning / 62
Tail Flaring / 63
Tail Wagging / 64
Beak Clicking / 65
Preening / 66

Playing / 68
Sleeping / 70
Head Bobbing / 72
Beak Grinding / 74

HAMSTERS

Grooming / 76
Stretching & Yawning / 78
Alert Ears / 79
Folded Back Ears / 80
Marking Territory / 81
Biting Their Cage / 82
Eyesight / 84
Hissing / 86
Burrowing / 87
Squeaks & Squeals / 88

GUINEA PIGS

Popcorning / 90
Touching Noses / 91
Running Away / 92
Wheeking / 93
Fidgeting / 94
Chutting / 96
Teeth Chattering / 97
Purring / 98
Rumbling & Rumble Strutting / 100
Scent Marking / 102

HORSES

Neighing or Whinnying / 104
Sighing / 106
Forward Ears / 107
Backward & Pinned Ears / 108
Nickering / 110
Raised Tail / 112
Fearful Tail / 113
Rapidly Swishing Tail / 114
Pawing / 115
Flehmen / 116

SNAKES

Tongue Flicking / 118
Head Wobbling / 120
Changing Eye Color / 121
S-Shape / 122
Yawning / 123
Musking / 124
Molting or Shedding / 126
Relaxed Behavior / 128
Curious Behavior / 129
Stressed Behavior / 130

FISH

Erratic Swimming / 132
Fin Nipping / 133
Glass Surfing / 134
Hiding / 136
Schools / 137
Gasping for Air / 138
Fish Aggression / 139
Digging / 140
Rapid Gill Movement / 142
Lack of Energy / 143

INTRODUCTION

Did you ever wish you knew what animals were trying to tell you? Now you can! In *How to Speak Animal*, you'll discover the dozens of ways that dogs, cats, rabbits, birds, hamsters, guinea pigs, horses, snakes, and fish communicate with their eyes, ears, bodies, movement, and, yes, voices!

You'll also find tons of extra tips to get the most out of your relationship with your animal:

 How to Speak: Once you know how an animal communicates, you can start figuring out how to speak back. The "How to Speak" boxes will provide simple tips on behaviors or sounds you can make that your animal will understand.

 Tips: You'll also learn extra tips about how to more deeply interpret animal behavior and provide the best caring environment.

 Did You Know? Some animals are just fascinating! You'll find extra tidbits in "Did You Know?" boxes to help you appreciate their unique characteristics.

Ready to unlock the secrets of the animal kingdom? From wheeking guinea pigs to periscoping rabbits, your journey begins now!

Dogs

1

THE PLAY BOW

The play bow is a way that dogs express to humans and other animals that it is playtime! It's a posture that dogs of all breeds and sizes use to communicate when they want to have fun. You'll know this position when your furry friend's front paws are outstretched, their chest is low to the ground, and their rear end is high in the air! Oftentimes their ears will be up and their tail wagging.

The play bow is an important signal to other dogs that his actions are amicable, especially when they are meeting for the first time. It's a good indicator that what might otherwise look like rough play is indeed friendly.

Speak Dog

Want to have some fun with your dog? You can try the play bow, too! Next time your dog is playful or shows you the play bow, simply copy their posture by bending at the waist and spreading out your arms. You'll have fun together in no time!

2

ROLLING OVER

A dog rolling over on her back to expose her belly is a sign of submission. When a dog is submissive, it means that they recognize that the other dog or human is "top dog" or "leader of the pack." Sometimes it can be a sign of respect, and other times it can be because she is scared. If she is scared or especially timid, you might also notice peeing accompanying the rolling over.

Maybe the dog just loves a good belly rub! Be sure to pay close attention to the situation and the dog's temperament. Never pet a dog's belly without much caution first. A dog rolled over is in its most vulnerable position because now it is exposed to attack, so be careful not to startle the dog, or you may get snapped. Always check that the dog is relaxed and comfortable with you, then rub away!

DOGS

EYE CONTACT

Have you ever heard the saying that eyes are windows to the soul? Well, it's just as true for dogs as it is for humans! Since dogs can't use words to communicate with us, they find other subtle ways to do so, especially with their eyes. Let's find out what they could be trying to say to you.

THE DIRECT STARE

The direct stare is a warning: beware! In this stare, the eyes are hard, direct, and tough. It means there could be a fight ahead if you don't back off. You may even notice the pupils dilating, which means the black part of the dog's eye getting larger and wider. Dogs use the rest of their body language as other good indicators of their feelings. Stay away from the dog if his tail is stiff (even if it's wagging), if his head is lowered, and if his body is still.

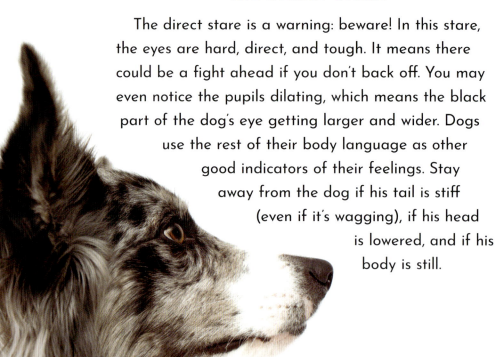

THE BEGGING STARE

If you notice a dog staring into the depths of your soul, chances are you have something she wants! This could be your food, her favorite toy, or simply a good scratch in her favorite spot. Sometimes this is referred to as "puppy dog eyes." This type of eye contact is a form of begging.

THE ADMIRING STARE

Most dogs love their people and just can't get enough of them. So they lovingly stare at them! It's the exact opposite of the direct stare. A dog's eyes will be soft and gentle, his tail might sweep back and forth, and his ears will be relaxed. He might even have a light pant. This is a sign of true admiration!

AVOIDANCE

Sometimes, dogs avoid eye contact altogether when they know they've done something naughty (like getting into the trash or chewing a shoe). Other times, they close their eyes because they're just really happy . . . and that belly rub feels so good! Remember, always look at the situation and environment for other clues to help you understand what a dog is trying to communicate to you.

TAIL POSTURE

dog's tail is one of the first things many people associate with a dog's demeanor.

WAGGING TAIL

The happy, wagging tail is easy to spot because it is in the shape of a U. The dog is relaxed and may even appear to be smiling, with a light pant. Some dogs even wiggle their entire booties in excitement! Their happiness is infectious and will surely make you smile as well.

TUCKED TAIL

A tail tucked between the rear legs is a sign that a dog is frightened or stressed. It's also a sign of submission, to show the dog doesn't want to fight. The tucked tail may also be accompanied by a lowered body and rolling over, belly-side up. Be slow and gentle around scared pups. You need to earn their trust before you can get close to them.

 Tip

If you see a dog with a tail that is held high (whether stiff or arching), be aware! It might just be alert to something, but the dog may also be dominant or aggressive and ready to attack. It is best to stay away.

DOGS

EAR LANGUAGE

Have you ever seen dogs tilt their head to one side or another when they hear the sound of your voice or something intriguing? It's pretty darn cute! Dogs, especially puppies, do this when they hear a new or peculiar sound and are trying to figure out where the sound is coming from. Perky, expressive ears tell us that a dog is highly focused.

DROOPY EARS

Droopy ears communicate that a dog may be submissive. Be careful not to confuse this with a dog that has naturally floppy ears. Dogs that are being submissive will hang their ears even lower than their natural, relaxed state. Remember, you'll also see the accompanying tucked tail between the rear legs.

DOGS

PINNED EARS

When a dog pins her ears back against her head, it could mean a few different things. Most likely, she is either fearful, nervous, or sad about something. Other times, dogs' ears go back to hear sounds that are coming from behind them.

Tip

How can you be sure whether a dog is scared or just listening to something? Always look for other clues and read his body language. Check for relaxed eyes, tail, mouth, and overall body stance.

6

NOSE & LIP LICKING

Have you ever noticed dogs licking their nose or lips when there isn't any food around? This is actually a really big signal to us humans! Nose and lip licking are what's known as an appeasement gesture. This is a type of submissive behavior. This means the dog is giving you what you want in order to keep you happy and keep things cordial between both of you. You may notice your dog doing this if you scold him. He's simply telling you that he isn't a threat to you. However, this doesn't mean that your dog understands why you were scolding him. Dogs are perceptive to our body language and tone of voice. Most likely, he's just anxious about your reaction. Dogs also use appeasement gestures with other dogs and animals. When meeting for the first time, one dog may lick its nose or lips as a way of saying, "I come in peace!"

> **Did You Know?**
>
> Just like human to human, yawns between humans and dogs are contagious! So if you see a dog yawn, you may soon find yourself yawning, too.

YAWNING

Yawning (outside of naptime and bedtime) is another type of appeasement gesture. Take notice! Many times, a misplaced yawn will be accompanied by lip licking. It's another way for a dog to deflect threats and avoid conflicts with humans and other dogs.

There is also the common yawn that we all know, because we do it, too! This is the sleepy yawn that dogs do when they are tired and need rest. It is a wide-open jaw accompanied by a deep, relaxing breath.

DOGS

23

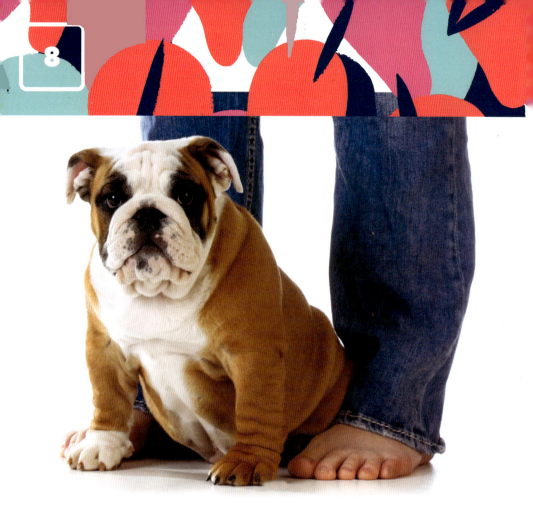

LEANING

If your dog leans on you or sits on your feet, it's a compliment: she loves you! Historically, dogs are pack animals. Since being domesticated (which means to tame an animal), dogs enjoy company and being physically close to their pack, which is usually their human family. But dogs can't cuddle the same as we do, so they put their body weight on or next to us. It's a sweet form of affection.

Big dogs in particular are known for putting all of their weight against your legs while you're standing. At times, it can almost push you over! While smaller dogs can be picked up and held much easier, larger dogs don't have the same advantage. Consequently, leaning is their way of being close to you.

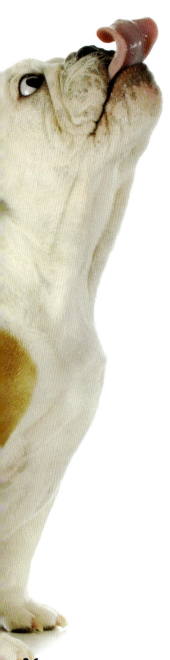

PEOPLE LICKING

Have you ever gotten puppy kisses? They might make you giggle, but have you ever wondered why dogs like to lick people?

TASTY TREAT

Our skin contains salt from our sweat. Our face and mouth may even contain food residue or crumbs. Yummy! All of those things sound pretty tasty to our four-legged friends.

AFFECTION

Licking can also be a form of affection. Notice your dog's body language. You'll know this type of licking when the dog is relaxed, their tail is wagging, and other signals of happiness are present. Licking is also very instinctual. Puppies are lovingly licked by their mother from birth. Puppies retain this habit as they grow and then carry it on as they mature into dogs.

APPEASEMENT

Licking can sometimes be an appeasement gesture. Dogs don't always know what we're saying, but they can sense our emotions. Dogs might try to appease our stress and anxiety or help calm us down if they feel like we are becoming too tense. Licking us also releases endorphins in their bodies (endorphins are happy chemicals that their bodies produce to relieve pain and stress). Whether you enjoy a sloppy wet kiss or not, in a dog's mind, it's a win-win!

10

REAR END SNIFFING

When dogs meet for the first time, they instantly sniff each other's rear ends. This is because they have incredible noses and can smell at least 10,000 times better than we do as humans. But why do they sniff such an awkward spot? Anal sacs located near each dog's rear end contain a ton of information, like the sex of the dog, diet, health, temperament, disposition, and even overall happiness. Dogs can learn a lot of information about each other in just minutes. This is their way of getting to know one another and it is completely normal dog behavior. There's no need to discourage it or be embarrassed by it!

Cats

TAILS

A cat's tail can really be one of the fastest ways to know what a cat is feeling.

AFFECTION

How do you know if a cat is approachable? If her tail curves down and then back up in a soft, gentle U-shape, she is relaxed. When cats hold their tail straight up, they are conveying a welcoming gesture. Sometimes the tip may even curl over like a bent finger as if to say, "Hello!" These cats are friendly and will likely accept a loving scratch or stroke down their backs.

Other outgoing cats will even greet you by wrapping their tails around your legs or with the tails of other cats. Much like a human's hug, this is a cat's version of a warm embrace. It's a way to show love and affection!

INTIMIDATION

A fluffy, puffed-up tail may look funny, but stay away! This kitty is scared of something. Cats fluff up their hair to make themselves look bigger and more intimidating if they feel threatened. If you hear hissing, it could also mean the cat is ready to attack as well. Back off!

Another cat to avoid is one that has its tail low to the ground or tucked between its legs. This poor kitty is scared and very nervous about something. If you get any closer, the claws and teeth may come out.

CURIOSITY

Have you ever noticed a cat's tail in the shape of a question mark? This is a sign that your cat is curious about something new and is ready to play. Now would be a good time to introduce a new toy.

12

THUMPING & FLICKING OF TAIL

Similar to dogs, cats also wag their tails, but it has a very different meaning.

THUMPING

Cats thump the ground with their tails when they want you to give them extra space. This thumping means that they have an increased level of alertness and agitation. They have become annoyed and want you to know that playtime is over.

FLICKING

Flicking, however, is different from thumping. You can tell it apart because most of the movement is only at the end or tip of the tail. It's a small, twitch-like motion. This indicates that the cat is hunting, playful, or is in the early stages of becoming annoyed.

EYES

Cats are known for being vague and confusing because they are much more independent than dogs. However, they really do send us quite a few clues to understand their mysterious language. We just have to realize what it is they are saying, and much of that is communicated through their eyes and eyelids.

NORMAL EYES

Alert, open eyes are a signal that a cat trusts you. Pupils, which are the black part of the eyes, will be at normal dilation and won't appear any larger or smaller. These types of eyes are often accompanied by cheek rubs, where the cat will headbutt the side of her face into you.

DILATED EYES

When a cat's pupils are large and dilated (i.e., you see a lot of black), the cat is stimulated. He could be stimulated by the excitement of a new toy or scared and fearful of something around him.

STARING EYES

Cats will often give an unblinking stare to other cats as a way to show control. They use it to display dominance over their important areas and territory. The unblinking stare is a warning signal.

SQUINTING EYES

A squinting cat with pupils that are narrow and constricted indicates a very aggressive cat. Cats that are very upset will often squint their eyes out of protection from a possible attack. Do not make eye contact with this cat! It could be perceived as a threat.

Speak Cat

If you see a cat giving you relaxed, droopy eyes, return her gaze and slowly blink. If she blinks back, congratulations! You have received a "kitty kiss" and this cat adores you.

14

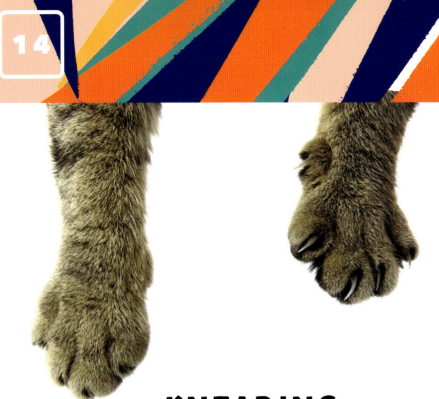

KNEADING

Have you ever made bread and kneaded the dough? That's where cat "kneading" gets its name. In fact, sometimes it's even called "making biscuits." Kneading is when a cat scrunches his paws into tiny fists and pushes a person or item rhythmically over and over with alternating paws.

Cat kneading is believed to be an old nursing habit that kittens use to stimulate milk production in their mothers. Kneading also releases scent glands located on the bottom of a cat's paws, marking the item or person he's kneading as his. Kneading is an action that very happy, contented cats make.

PURRING

When a kitten is born, it cannot hear and its eyes are not yet open. The mother kitten purrs to her babies so they can find her and her milk. Although they cannot hear the purring, they can feel the deep vibration. Within just two days after being born, kittens are then able to purr in response. Purring is often done while a kitten is kneading to stimulate an increase in its mother's milk.

Kittens continue to purr as grown cats when they are relaxed, happy, and showing affection to another cat or human. It is certainly one of the most obvious signs of your cat's pleasure! But did you know that cats also purr when they're hurt or in pain? Some research shows that purring actually helps cats get better faster!

16

MEOWING

Kittens are born with their eyes shut and ear canals closed, so they meow for their mothers when they need their care. But as kittens grow and mature, meowing becomes a language used almost exclusively for humans. Meowing is a cat's way to tell you her wants and needs. Most often, it is to express hunger, her need to go outside, or her desire for attention.

Tip

The tone and length of the meow will provide you with a lot of information. If a cat gives a short, high-pitched meow, the cat is happy. The lower and more stretched out the meow, the more demanding and annoyed the cat is.

BUTT PRESENTATION

When cats approach each other in a friendly way, they will often hold their tail straight up and rub against each other. Then, the cats will proceed to sniff each other's scent glands, which are located near the cats' rear ends. These scent glands provide detailed information about the cats' health, diet, and lifestyle, which enables the cats to quickly get to know one another. So, when your cat rubs against you and then proceeds to stick his rear end near your face, it's his way of asking for a rub and sharing his scent with you. It means he trusts you as a friend and that he's reaffirming that you are a part of his pack.

LICKING

Cats spend an enormous amount of time licking themselves, also known as self-grooming. In fact, they spend up to half of their time awake licking themselves. It's not just to look pretty, but it's also how they keep clean and healthy. A cat's tongue has a rough surface, made up of numerous papillae that are like tiny backward-facing hooks. Many people describe it as feeling like sandpaper. These papillae help grab the fur and comb through it, spreading out the sebum oil naturally produced on the cat's skin. This also removes dirt and other debris from the cat's fur, keeping it clean and naturally shiny from the oil.

In other areas where the tongue can't reach (such as the face), a cat will lick her forepaw to dampen it and then proceed to clean the area with her paw.

Cats will even lick and groom one another if they have a friendly relationship. They typically do this to help their friend get to those hard-to-reach areas like the back of the neck or head.

Tip

If you have a cat that adores you, he may lick you as a sign of affection. It may not always feel good, but he's showing you that you are part of his family and part of his territory. Simply stated, he cares for you!

CATS

19

HUNTING

Cats, even domesticated ones, are born to hunt. They enjoy the thrill of the chase, and occasionally they just can't resist the urge to hunt. Cats that catch prey (usually a lizard, bird, or mouse) will show off their prize and bring it to their owners as a gift. This is because cats are pack animals and share the rewards of their hunt with their pack—you! As gross as it may seem to you, this is a sign your cat loves you.

Indoor cats that have a natural drive to hunt can also make very playful cats. Their brains, in particular, need extra stimulation to fulfill their desire to chase and catch their prey. You'll find that they have instinctual prey-drive behavior that appears in

play form. For example, they love to pounce on feet walking by, chase laser pointers, or attack feather toys. These are all activities that are fulfilling their prey drive.

Speak Cat

When a cat brings you some prey he hunted, don't scold him! Instead, show affection and appreciation. He'll know you're pleased with his gift!

BELLY UP

A cat will only roll on her back when she is most relaxed and feels safe and secure. Similar to dogs, when a cat is on her back with her belly up, she exposes herself to attack. This is the most vulnerable position for a cat. If your cat does this, she's happy and wants some attention from you. But be careful not to pet the belly, as most cats will scratch you if you attempt that. Aim for her favorite places, like under the chin or a good scratch on the ears.

Other reasons your cat may be rolling over is to mark her territory by rubbing her scent on the ground. Or, maybe she's just scratching an itch on her back!

Rabbits

LOAFING

Loafing is one of the most common rabbit positions, and it's pretty easy to spot, too. Loafing is often nicknamed the "bunny loaf" because the rabbit looks like a little round loaf of bread. It's actually rather adorable!

When they do this, rabbits tuck all four legs completely underneath their bodies, slick back their ears, and squint or close their eyes. A loafing rabbit means she is relaxed and lounging. It also means she trusts her environment and the people in it. Rabbits will even sleep in this position, especially if it is cold. Some rabbits prefer this position to flopping or sprawling.

FLOPPING & SPRAWLING

FLOPPING

Rabbit flopping is a motion in which a rabbit lies on his side with his eyes closed and his legs very still. A rabbit in this posture is very relaxed, contented, and trusting. Rabbits flop over to their side in calm environments where they feel safe and secure.

SPRAWLING

Sprawling is similar to flopping. This is when your rabbit is stretched out on the floor or ground in a relaxed manner, but she is not flopped on her side. Instead, she is on her belly. She may even rest her head on her front legs. Sprawling is a sign that your rabbit is getting comfortable with you.

 Tip

Take note if your pet rabbit doesn't flop over in front of you. This may be a good indicator that the two of you need more bonding time together.

Tip

A scared bunny doesn't periscope—it hides. So if your pet rabbit is periscoping with more frequency, congratulations! This means it is beginning to gain confidence and feel more secure in its environment.

PERISCOPING

Periscoping is another rabbit trait that makes them almost irresistible! This is when a rabbit stands up on his hind legs. Rabbits do this to look farther ahead, gain a better vantage point, or reach something up high.

BINKYING & ZOOMING

abbits are very dramatic little creatures. When they get excited, it bottles up until they just can't hold it in anymore.

BINKYING

Sometimes they express their enthusiasm through jumping, kicking, and twisting movements that look like dancing! These funny, entertaining actions are called binkying, and may be accompanied by dashing and zooming around the room. Binkying is different from regular jumping, as it is more sporadic and includes unpredictable movements with the back legs.

ZOOMING

Zooming is another type of energy burst that rabbits may exhibit. Also known as the "Bunny 500," zooming is when your rabbit races in circles around the room. But don't worry! Zooming is another characteristic of a happy, playful, and excited rabbit.

PURRING

Yes, it's true that rabbits purr! But unlike cats, a rabbit's purr does not come from her throat—it actually comes from her teeth. A rabbit will gently grind her teeth together, creating a soft vibration in her head. Similar to cats, the vibrating purring sound means that your rabbit is very calm, happy, and content.

However, if you notice your rabbit's teeth-grinding becoming very loud and frequent, this could be a good indicator that your rabbit is in pain. Look for other clues to help you determine the difference. A purring rabbit will be relaxed, flopped over, or lying in your lap with legs extended. A rabbit grinding its teeth in pain will be tense, hunched over, and could possibly show signs of aggression or avoidance of food.

ALERT POSTURE & EARS

When a rabbit gets alerted, you'll see his body posture become tense. His eyes widen and nose rapidly twitches, trying to detect all possible threats approaching. Sometimes he remains on all four legs, and other times he might stand in the periscoping position. Either way, he is ready to dash off at a moment's notice.

You can also know if your rabbit is afraid by looking at his ears. His ears become alert and turn in different directions if he senses danger or potential threats. In fact, each ear can rotate 270 degrees, even without moving the rest of his body! This gives him the ability to detect exactly where the sound is coming from.

27

GROOMING

Grooming is an essential part of a rabbit's everyday life. Rabbits groom their entire body multiple times a day. This helps them stay clean, with a sleek and shiny coat. To do this, they clean their head by licking their front paws and then using them to wipe their face and ears. They clean the rest of their body by bending around and licking it clean with their tongues.

If you have two or more rabbits living together and they become bonded, they will even begin to groom one another. This is a sign of affection between rabbits. One rabbit licking another proves that she cares about her hygiene and cleanliness. Licking and bonded grooming is also a sign of a dominant rabbit. You'll know which rabbit is dominant by watching to see who receives the most licks from the others.

Did You Know?

Rabbits cannot vomit. This means that unlike cats, rabbits do not have hair balls. When a rabbit grooms himself, the hair passes through his digestive system.

28

CAUTIOUS BEHAVIOR

This is an incredibly common rabbit behavior. A cautious rabbit will move slowly and carefully around a space, often tiptoeing like a ninja! She will stop frequently to look and listen to her surroundings. She might stretch out her body as far as she can with her back feet staying in the same place. Keeping her back feet planted firmly on the ground gives her the ability to make a run for it if she gets scared.

Tip

It is common for rabbits to display cautious behavior when they enter a new room or place that they are hesitant about. They may also act like this when they encounter new people or objects that they just aren't quite sure of yet.

RABBITS

29

THUMPING

Thumping is the loudest sound a rabbit makes. Imagine hearing a loud *thud* on the ground, as if you dropped a heavy book. That is almost exactly what thumping sounds like! Rabbits make this loud noise by hitting their hind legs hard against the ground or floor. People who have grown up watching the movie *Bambi* as kids believe that thumping means a happy, contented bunny. That couldn't be further from the truth!

Speak Rabbit

If your rabbit is thumping while hunkered down with his ears bent, he is thumping because he is scared. This is an appropriate time to comfort your rabbit and help reassure him that everything will be all right. You can do this by stroking or holding him and speaking softly.

Thumping is actually a way a rabbit warns others of the dangers he perceives (whether that danger is you or something else). It also could mean that the rabbit is upset with you, so be careful!

If your pet rabbit is thumping, this could also be a sign that he wants more attention from you. Think of a human toddler throwing a temper tantrum. It's his way to throw a fit! Be careful not to give in and reward his bad behavior, especially with treats. Pay attention to his body language, his eyes, and the position in which he holds his ears. If he is thumping simply for attention, your rabbit will have confident body language.

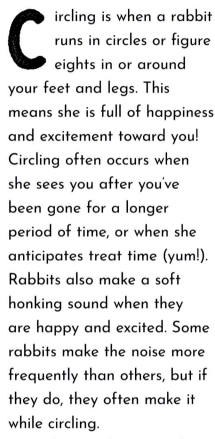

CIRCLING

Circling is when a rabbit runs in circles or figure eights in or around your feet and legs. This means she is full of happiness and excitement toward you! Circling often occurs when she sees you after you've been gone for a longer period of time, or when she anticipates treat time (yum!). Rabbits also make a soft honking sound when they are happy and excited. Some rabbits make the noise more frequently than others, but if they do, they often make it while circling.

Circling is also a way for some rabbits to get your attention. They might be hungry or just need some extra affection.

Birds

EYE PINNING

Eye pinning, also known as eye flashing, is a unique characteristic to birds. This is when a bird dilates its pupils (the black part of the eye) from large to small. It repeats this pattern back and forth, from large to small, as long as he is stimulated.

Eye pinning is most likely to occur when the bird is excited or becoming aggressive. How do you know which stimuli he's feeling? If he's excited, you may notice pinning eyes and relaxed feathers. You may even get some head bobs. Depending on the species, this could be a good time to teach a new trick. If, on the other hand, he's feeling aggressive, look for signs such as pinning eyes and the spreading out of his wings. He may even try to bite you, so be careful.

TAIL FLARING

Tail flaring is when a bird spreads out his tail sideways. This action is also referred to as tail fanning, because the tail looks like the shape of a fan. Birds do this in order to appear larger than they really are. Upright posture and eye pinning will often accompany this behavior. Tail flaring is an aggressive form of body language that releases tension. Be aware! Tail flaring is a signal that the bird may bite you if you continue the activity that caused the fanning.

BIRDS

TAIL WAGGING

Tail wagging looks just as it sounds: a quick wag to the right and left of a bird's tail. Similar to a dog, tail wagging in a bird means the bird is happy and having fun! Birds most often wag their tails when they see their favorite person or during a fun activity with a favorite toy.

Careful not to confuse tail wagging with tail flaring, because these body languages actually have opposite meanings.

Also, some birds wag their tails just before defecating (or pooping). This might seem weird, but it's really helpful to know if you have a pet bird that you want to house-train to use the bathroom on command.

34

BEAK CLICKING

Beak clicking is a fast, sharp clicking noise a bird makes. Most commonly, she will tap the tip of her upper beak over the bottom beak to make this noise. However, some species will use their tongues, and others even make the noise in their throat. For some birds, beak clicking means that they are in an excited state. Usually, though, beak clicking is a sign that the bird is feeling threatened and her way of saying, "Back off!"

BIRDS

35

PREENING

Did you know that a bird has between 1,500 and 3,000 feathers, depending on the species? This makes preening—a bird's way of cleaning her feathers—an essential task. A healthy bird will spend a great deal of her time preening, so it's important to understand what she's doing.

Preening is how birds keep their feathers clean, waterproof, insulated, and in flying condition.

Tip

If your bird isn't preening, it might be ill or in an uncomfortable living situation.

Most birds have a special preen gland located at the base of the tail. This gland produces an oily substance that birds spread across their feathers. It acts as weatherproofing against water and also keeps the bird's feathers from becoming brittle and breaking. Have you ever seen what looks like a bird pecking at her back? She's actually using her beak to get the oil from her back and spread it onto every feather. It's a very labor-intensive process!

Birds also have a naturally occurring dust that forms close to their bodies around certain types of feathers. Birds will use their beaks to break up this powdery substance and then spread it across their feathers. This dust acts as an additional form of weatherproofing. When she is done preening, your bird may give herself a good fluff and a shake. You'll likely notice a cloud of dust during this shake. Now you know where all of that is coming from!

Birds that live in the same flock, whether in the wild or in a cage, may lovingly preen one another. This is a sign that they have bonded. They will do this for especially hard-to-reach areas like the tops of their heads.

PLAYING

Did you know that, just like you, birds like to play? Birds are actually very intelligent creatures and can get bored sitting in a cage. They really enjoy playing with toys, as it stimulates brain and physical activity.

If birds live in a group, you might also see them playing together. Birds often play by mouthing each other. Some people refer to this activity as "bird jousting" because it looks like the birds are wrestling with their beaks. It's all in good fun and the birds aren't injured in the process. After jousting, the bonded birds will often preen each other—an act of true friendship!

🔊 Speak Bird

In the wild, many birds make up their own songs. You can make up songs to sing for your bird, too! They'll love hearing your voice, and the mental stimulation is good for them.

SLEEPING

Birds take many naps throughout the day. Did you know that many species nap standing on one leg? This shows that the bird feels safe and secure in her environment. You may begin to hear beak grinding as the bird settles down for her slumber. She may even turn her head around and tuck it into her back feathers. A bird snuggled up for a nap is adorable!

However, if your bird is napping on both legs with her feathers fluffed out, it's actually an indication that she could be cold or even sick. If this continues, seek veterinary care.

💡 *Tip*

Birds require 10-12 hours of uninterrupted sleep at night. Much like us humans, if they don't get quality sleep, they can become cranky! Many people choose to cover their cages at night to ensure darkness and to eliminate sleep distractions.

BIRDS

HEAD BOBBING

Head bobbing is a normal part of a pet bird's body language. Head bobbing, along with moving his head from side to side, is his way of getting your attention. This is especially true in some species like parrots. It's like they're saying, "Hellloooooooo, over here!"

Some birds dance and head bob to get your attention, and others do this to music they love. Dancing and head bobbing to music can be a trained technique. This is actually one of the easiest tricks for some birds to learn, especially cockatiels and parrots. They are smarter than you may have otherwise believed!

Male parakeets will bob their heads up and down in efforts to find a mate. They are trying to impress the ladies! They head bob while doing a little dance, and this gets the attention of the females in the area. Other birds may bob their heads out of aggression if they feel their territory is being threatened. Look for other body language clues, like flared tail feathers, ruffled feathers, and pinning eyes, to determine if this is the case. If it is, it's best to stay away.

BEAK GRINDING

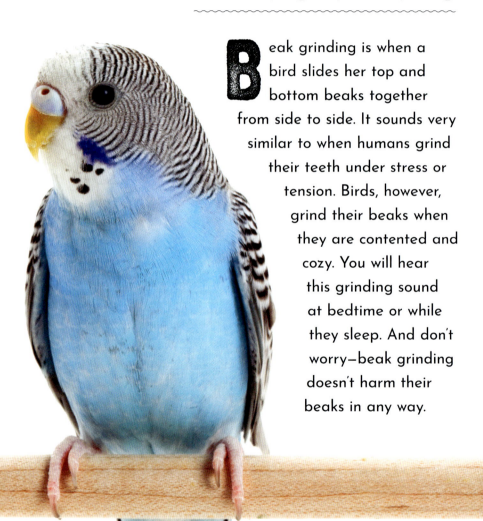

Beak grinding is when a bird slides her top and bottom beaks together from side to side. It sounds very similar to when humans grind their teeth under stress or tension. Birds, however, grind their beaks when they are contented and cozy. You will hear this grinding sound at bedtime or while they sleep. And don't worry—beak grinding doesn't harm their beaks in any way.

Hamsters

GROOMING

Grooming is a hamster's way of cleaning his fur and paws. Hamsters groom themselves by licking their bodies with their tongues. For hard-to-reach areas, for example his head, he will lick his front paws and then wipe the paws on his head until clean.

Hamsters are very detailed with their grooming habits. However, a hamster will not groom himself when he feels threatened or unsafe. Instead, he stays alert and hides. So if you see a hamster grooming himself regularly, this hamster feels safe, secure, and content. He will also be clean and healthy!

Have you ever heard the saying "too much of a good thing"? This is the case if your hamster becomes preoccupied with cleaning himself. This could be a sign that your hamster has a skin issue, or simply that your hamster is nervous or afraid and is trying to calm his anxiety. Either way, it is best to take precaution and see a veterinarian when this happens.

STRETCHING & YAWNING

Stretching and yawning are two of the most common hamster behaviors. When humans stretch and yawn, usually it's because we are sleepy or have just woken up. But interestingly enough, that's not usually the case with hamsters! When a hamster yawns and stretches out her body and legs, it's actually conveying the message that she's relaxed, content, and happy.

ALERT EARS

Did you know that hamsters are prey animals? This means that they have many predators in the wild. To keep them safe from harm, they are always on the lookout, watching and listening to their surroundings.

When a hamster is in this alert mode, he has his ears forward and may even sit up on his hind legs. This helps him to be able to listen intently. Alert ears help the hamster collect as much information as possible about potential predators and other nearby threats.

You can also look for other body language clues to help you determine if your hamster has alert ears. Puffed up cheek pouches is another signal that your hamster feels insecure. If this is the case, give your hamster some time to feel a bit more confident with his surroundings before handling him.

FOLDED BACK EARS

After a hard playtime or run on the wheel, your hamster may be exhausted! (Aren't you after playing and exercising?) This is typically when a hamster will tiredly fold her ears back. It's a sign she needs a break, and it's best to respect her need for space. Other times, you might see her ears folded back when she is very nervous or suspicious of you. To tell the difference, look at her eyes. When she is afraid, they will be narrowed and focused. This hamster is fearful! Don't reach for her or you may get bit.

MARKING TERRITORY

Hamsters are territorial animals. This means that they protect the area where they live from the invasion of other species. How do they do this?

Depending on the species, hamsters have a unique scent gland located near their hip or stomach area. They rub this part of their body on different objects in their cage (or wherever they consider home), which leaves behind their scent. Now they have officially marked that object or space as their own.

Have you ever held a hamster and noticed that it began grooming itself afterward? It was removing your scent! Hamsters prefer to not smell like anything but themselves.

HAMSTERS

45

BITING THEIR CAGE

If you see a hamster biting the bars of his cage, this is a cause for concern. If your hamster begins this behavior, it is often a sign that he wants more attention. First, examine how often he is getting let out of his cage. Playtime, exercise, and socialization are very important for hamsters. Is this happening at least once a day or is the time out of the cage too short? Try increasing the frequency or duration of time that you spend with your hamster out of the cage. This may eliminate the behavior.

If more attention doesn't solve the problem, he may need something to chew. Did you know that a hamster's four front teeth never stop growing? If not properly taken care of, a hamster's teeth can become overgrown, or even worse, they can grow into the gums or roof of his mouth. Sounds awful, right? In worst-case scenarios, a vet can trim his teeth, but it's better to prevent this from happening altogether.

Tip

Quality, hard food will help maintain your hamster's teeth. But if he is biting his cage, you should also add a special wood block that is made specifically for small pets to gnaw on.

HAMSTERS

EYESIGHT

Did you know that hamsters have very poor eyesight? In fact, because they live in dark burrows in the wild, they can really only see a couple of inches past their noses! As a result, hamsters rely on their hearing and sense of smell to be able to get around and keep safe. At home, they don't recognize you visually or know what you look like. However, they do know your scent and recognize your voice.

Speak Hamster

Because of her poor eyesight, you must alert a hamster that you're there by talking to her first. Move slowly and gently. Place your hand in the cage, palm side up. Allow the hamster to climb on you, and then you can gently scoop her up. This will help your hamster feel more comfortable and will avoid startling her.

HISSING

Hissing is the loudest sound that hamsters make. Sure enough, it sounds similar to a snake's hiss, hence the name! Hissing is a hamster's way of protecting himself. Anytime he becomes alarmed or senses danger, he will hiss to scare away predators. If a hamster is not in hiding, look for other body language signals that show he is being protective. These may include the hamster crouching down, opening his mouth wide to show his teeth, or raising his front paws while hissing. These are all behaviors that you want to avoid. Be careful and keep away!

BURROWING

Hamsters naturally like to burrow in the wild. They build intricate tunnel systems to store food, find cooler temperatures underground, and protect themselves. Burrowing is instinctual, so pet hamsters will want to burrow as well. This is good, since it's also good exercise for them, and many enjoy sleeping while burrowed.

To encourage burrowing behaviors, make sure your hamster has plenty of space. Some people even provide a separate, larger enclosure specifically for burrowing. Your hamster will need bedding at least seven inches deep. Once the space is ready to go, sit back and watch him get to work tunneling!

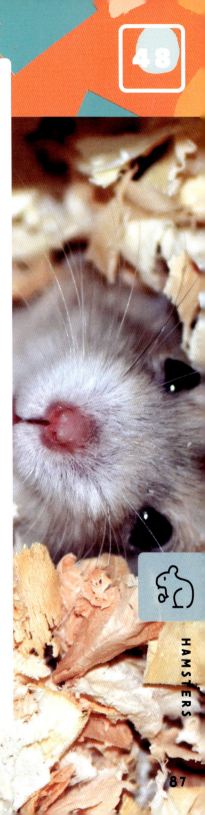

49

SQUEAKS & SQUEALS

Hamsters are fairly quiet pets, and squeaking and squealing is the most common sound that you will hear. Each hamster is different, though. Some hamsters squeak and squeal in delight with a treat or during playtime. But for the most part, squeaks and squeals mean a hamster is frightened, agitated, or possibly in pain.

While it is common for hamsters to squeak for the first few days in a new cage, they are typically quiet after that. It may also happen when startling the hamster or holding her with insecure hands. If the squeak or squeal grows in volume or frequency, you need to look for context clues to determine the root cause and respect your hamster's desire to be left alone.

Guinea Pigs

POPCORNING

Popcorning happens in moments of joy that guinea pigs express through jumping. Popcorning gets its name because it looks quite similar to little corn kernels popping into popcorn. For guinea pigs, these small jumps can happen from the standing position or while a guinea pig is walking. They may change direction and squeak with excitement. Your guinea pig is so happy, she can't contain herself!

Popcorning is most common with younger guinea pigs. The older and larger a guinea pig grows, the more challenging it is to popcorn due to size and weight. As with humans, some excitement and enthusiasm also wears off after a guinea pig reaches puberty. While many guinea pigs will popcorn their entire lives (just maybe not as high), if your aging guinea pig slowly stops, it shouldn't be a reason for concern.

TOUCHING NOSES

Touching noses is most often a friendly and sometimes affectionate greeting given by guinea pigs. Guinea pigs will touch noses to their cage mates and also to their favorite humans. Think of this as similar to how humans shake hands, wave, or bow in some cultures. It's a nice way to greet each other and say, "Hello!"

GUINEA PIGS

52

RUNNING AWAY

Guinea pigs are naturally timid animals. This is especially true at first with a new pet guinea. Guinea pigs will often run away from you as you attempt to pick them up. Try not to take offense or get sad about this; it doesn't mean they are personally rejecting you. Guinea pigs are naturally a prey animal. They use running away as a defense mechanism to keep themselves safe and alive. With time, your guinea pig will get used to (and even love!) you picking him up and cuddling.

WHEEKING

Wheeking is perhaps the trademark of guinea pigs, because it's such a distinguishable characteristic. It is the most common sound a guinea pig makes. Wheeking is a high-pitched squeak and sounds just like how you pronounce the name.

In the wild, guinea pigs wheek to fellow guinea pigs to alert them to danger. But in captivity, guinea pigs only wheek to humans.

Wheeking actually means your guinea pig is really excited! Oftentimes, when you hear this noise, your guinea may also begin running around inside his pen. If he has cage mates, they will likely all begin wheeking. Pretty soon you'll have a guinea pig wheeking choir! Guineas pigs most often wheek in anticipation for food.

FIDGETING

Fidgeting is a common issue with new pet guinea pigs. When you handle them, you might notice them squirming a lot. This could mean a couple of things. First, guinea pigs do not like to defecate (go to the bathroom) on their owners. They may need a break in their cage to allow them some time to take care of their business.

If that doesn't solve the problem and the fidgeting persists, your guinea pig is trying to let you know that she is tired of being held. As always, it's best to watch and respect these body signals.

CHUTTING

Chutting is a sound that guinea pigs make when they are enjoying life. This noise is sometimes referred to as "clucking" or "croaking" because it can sound similar to both words when pronounced softly.

Guinea pigs usually chutt when they are running around or exploring. Chutting is their way of talking to themselves. In essence, they are so relaxed and content, they don't care who hears them!

Tip

Chutting usually occurs during their daily habits, but it may also occur toward you while you hold them.

TEETH CHATTERING

Chattering is a sound guinea pigs make when they quickly clank their teeth together. While you may think your guinea pig is cold, unlike humans, guinea pigs don't actually chatter in chilly temperatures. So what's going on? It's actually a pretty aggressive form of body language that guinea pigs use. It means, "Back off!" or, "Stay away or else there could be a fight." Some guinea pigs will show their teeth during chattering, which looks similar to a yawn. If you encounter a guinea pig with chattering teeth, back away and leave it alone.

PURRING

A guinea pig's purr can be pretty confusing. While a purring cat means it is content, a purring guinea pig isn't so straightforward. Purring can mean opposite things in guinea pigs. If you listen closely, though, you'll notice the differences in their sounds.

If a guinea pig makes a low purring sound, he is content and relaxed. This usually occurs during treat time or playtime. He is communicating to you that he is happy!

But if a guinea pig makes a higher-pitched purr, particularly at the end of the purr, the guinea pig is annoyed. His body may even tense up and vibrate. He is ready to be left alone and is communicating to you that he is not happy.

Tip

Guinea pigs will sometimes purr when they are afraid. This is a very quick purr that is sometimes called a durr. The guinea pig may freeze and remain still. It may also be accompanied by a high squeak.

RUMBLING & RUMBLE STRUTTING

Rumbling is a very low sound a guinea pig makes when she is very upset. This sound is sometimes referred to as "motor boating." It is deep and sounds similar to an engine, and there are many different reasons it might happen.

DOMINANCE

Guinea pigs will rumble toward each other as a sign of dominance. This is especially common in groups of guinea pigs. In the event that the rumbling becomes aggressive, place a towel or blanket over them. Guinea pigs become so distracted worrying how to escape that they usually forget about fighting altogether.

ATTRACTION

Other times, a male guinea pig might rumble when he is trying to attract a female guinea pig during mating. You can differentiate this rumbling sound from the others because it will be combined with a rumble strut. Rumble strutting is a mating dance used by the males to attract the females. It looks like the guinea pig is shaking its booty from side to side as it rumbles.

FERTILITY

Lastly, female guinea pigs will also rumble during the time of the month when they could become pregnant.

59

SCENT MARKING

Like other territorial animals, guinea pigs will claim spaces and items. You can identify this behavior when you see a guinea pig rubbing his chin or cheeks on an object he wants to claim. Guinea pigs also drag their bottom, leaving behind their scent, which marks an area as their territory. Sometimes, guinea pigs will even urinate in areas or on other guinea pigs that they want to have dominance over. As disgusting as it sounds, it's normal behavior for them. Keeping their cage clean will help reduce or eliminate any foul smells.

Tip

You can't stop scent marking, but you can reduce the odor by keeping the cage clean.

Horses

NEIGHING OR WHINNYING

Neighing is often referred to as whinnying. Children are taught from a young age that horses neigh, but neighing is actually one of the least common sounds a horse makes. Do you even know what it means? Most people don't!

A horse typically only neighs or whinnies to other horses. It's asking, "Where are you?" When you hear a horse neigh, you will likely hear another horse neigh in response, "Over here!" Incredibly, the sound of a horse's neigh can be heard from about a quarter mile away. Horses will neigh and whinny to each other when they become separated or if they are in a new environment (such as a horse show or trail ride) and want to find out what other horses are around.

Did You Know?

Horses from the same herd make similar sounds! Humans speak in accents and have different speaking patterns based on regions where they live, and horses are the same. If you listen to multiple horses neigh, you will hear the differences in their tone, depth, and duration.

HORSES

105

SIGHING

Take in a big, deep breath and hold it. Now, exhale through your nose. That's what a horse sounds like when they sigh, only louder! Horses sigh quite often, such as while being groomed, receiving special care like a massage, or while being ridden. Sighing can mean they are relaxed, content, or bored, or can even be a release of tension.

FORWARD EARS

One of the most important things to learn about a horse's body language is the position of its ears. Generally speaking, if the ears are relaxed while facing forward, the horse is alert, paying attention, and interested in what is in front of it. If the ears become tense and stiff, though, the horse is now alarmed and potentially nervous about something ahead.

What if you see a horse with its ears turned out to the side? Well, this horse is actually just asleep or relaxed.

Speak Horse

Before approaching a horse, softly call her name and make some noise. This will tell her that you are nearby.

HORSES

BACKWARDS & PINNED EARS

When a horse's ears are pinned back close to the neck, the horse is angry and you should stay away. This horse could bite or kick!

Other times, horses will have their ears turned backward, but they won't necessarily be pinned against their necks. This just means that they're listening to sounds behind them (in order to hear better, they turn their ears in that direction). Just to be sure, look for other body language clues. If a horse is upset, you'll also see a swishing tail and a tense body.

Lastly, you may on occasion see a horse with swiveling ears. This is when a horse is trying to locate the sound of something alarming. He will quickly move his ears from forward to backward, back and forth, creating a swiveling effect. This horse is anxious and alert and might easily become spooked. Be cautious!

NICKERING

A nicker is a soft, low-pitched sound that horses commonly make. Nickers have a deep sound because they are made using a horse's vocal cords while the mouth remains shut. Nickers are short in length, but you'll probably hear multiple in succession, one right after another. Nickers have three distinct meanings, each based on the situation.

GREETING NICKER

The most frequent nicker you will hear is classified as the greeting nicker. This is when two horses meet or when a horse sees one of his favorite humans. It is the sound of a friendly horse greeting, as if to say, "Hello there, good to see you." You'll also notice that the horse will have a raised head, pricked ears, and may nudge you with his nose. Some horses also nicker when they see their favorite food.

COURTSHIP NICKER

A stallion (an adult male horse that can be used for breeding) will also nicker to a mare (an adult female horse) as part of his courtship ritual. Each stallion has a uniquely different pulse rate in their nicker, and interestingly enough, a mare is able to identify the stallion just by listening. She doesn't even need to turn to see him!

WARNING NICKER

Mares will also nicker to their foals (baby horses under the age of one) to warn them of danger. This nicker means "come closer" and is very soft and quiet. It tells the foal to stay near her. Foals never need to be taught this special warning; they simply know this from birth!

65

RAISED TAIL

A raised tail, sometimes called a "flagged" tail, is when the tail is carried high above the back of the horse. This indicates the horse is excited, very energized, and happy. This is especially common in young foals who love to run and express their playfulness. A raised tail can be easily confused with breeds that have a naturally higher tail carriage, such as Arabians.

FEARFUL TAIL

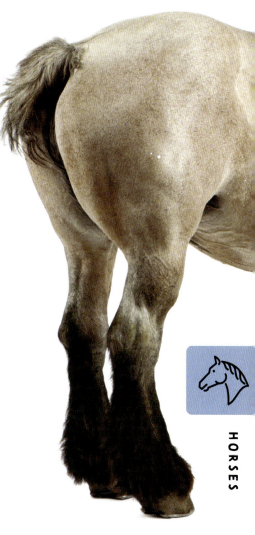

Horses express fear and submission through their tails just like dogs do. If nervous or stressed, horses will tuck their tail down tight to their bodies close between their hindquarters. This horse needs calm reassurance. If you notice this behavior while riding, stop and check all of your tack (saddle and other horse gear) to make sure it fits correctly. Move away from loud, new, or uncertain areas, which may cause uneasiness in a horse. If this body language persists with no obvious reason as to why, call your veterinarian.

HORSES

67

RAPIDLY SWISHING TAIL

It is normal for horses to lightly swish their tails. This is actually very useful at keeping the flies away! *Rapid* swishing of a tail, though, is more of a fast, jerking motion. It can be side to side or up and down. This means that the horse is angry and you should stay away! Horses that are angry can kick, buck, or bite you at any moment.

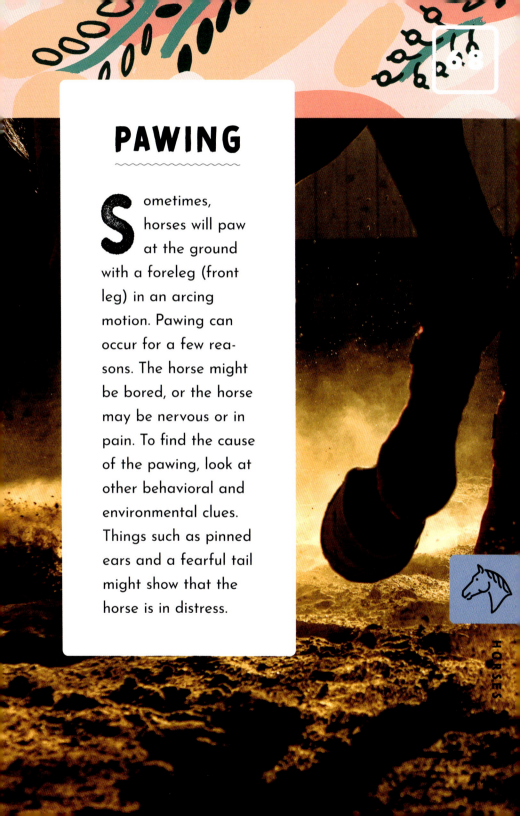

PAWING

Sometimes, horses will paw at the ground with a foreleg (front leg) in an arcing motion. Pawing can occur for a few reasons. The horse might be bored, or the horse may be nervous or in pain. To find the cause of the pawing, look at other behavioral and environmental clues. Things such as pinned ears and a fearful tail might show that the horse is in distress.

FLEHMEN

Have you ever seen any funny pictures of horses with their teeth showing? No, they're not smiling for the camera! That's actually called flehmen, and it's the word used to describe a natural response to enhance a horse's sense of smell. The horse will raise and stretch his neck forward, roll his upper lip back to display his teeth, inhale, and then blow the air back out. This entertaining process is rather funny-looking, but it's pretty helpful. When the horse pushes the air back out, it actually goes through a special structure in his nose that detects chemicals in the air. Horses will do this if there's something new they're curious about and they want more information.

Snakes

70

TONGUE FLICKING

Have you ever thought a snake flicking its tongue was creepy or maybe even a little scary? Well, it turns out that a snake's tongue isn't meant to look threatening at all. In fact, it's actually helping the snake smell! Snakes have very limited vision and hearing, so they rely heavily on their sense of smell.

When a snake flicks his tongue, he picks up tiny scent particles in the air. These scent particles then go to the roof of his mouth, where a special organ called the Jacobson's organ is located. This organ sends messages to the brain that tell the snake what the scent particles are. Pretty crazy, right?

Tip

If a snake begins to have short, quick tongue flicks, she has become distracted. Food is likely the cause, such as a mouse, but if this is the case, the snake will bite at it. Be careful and aware by always watching the snake so you can be prepared.

SNAKES

119

HEAD WOBBLING

A head wobble can be found in any snake during meal time. This happens when they get excited or smell something new. Typically, it will look like a back-and-forth movement. However, some breeds of snakes will get a different type of head wobble. The Spider Morph Ball Python has a type of head wobble that is best described as more of a corkscrew, as the snake can end up backward and upside down rather than just moving side to side. The snake will sway and lose coordination. He may become disoriented and have difficulty eating due to the head wobble. While it is sad to watch snakes with this condition, it in no way harms them.

So, what causes such a dramatic head wobble in some snakes? It has been determined that it is not genetics, but beyond that, little is known. It requires a patient and skilled handler to work with these snakes.

CHANGING EYE COLOR

Did you know that a snake's eye color can change? Specifically, it can become cloudy and take on a gray-blue tint. It looks pretty cool (or pretty freaky, depending on how big of a reptile fan you are), and this is a sign that the snake is about ready to shed her skin. Here's what happens. As her old skin loosens, a fluid builds up in between the old and new skin. It also builds up in the snake's eyes, which explains the color you are seeing. Something else that's really neat is that this cloudy bluish liquid actually makes the snake almost blind. During the peak of this pre-shedding time, you'll notice the pupils will be completely invisible behind this liquid. Once the snake reabsorbs this liquid, her eyes go back to normal and her vision does, too. Pretty cool!

SNAKES

73

S-SHAPE

Snakes are quite flexible and can bend and move in many ways. But a very important shape to know about is the S-shape. When the neck coils into this curved stance, it's a sign the snake will strike. She may not strike right away, but this pose should not be dismissed. She is ready to defend herself at any moment and will! Remember, too, that snakes can strike from any position (not just the S-shape), so always be careful.

YAWNING

Yawning, also called mouth gaping, is a rather cute behavior that snakes will sometimes do, but it may not mean what you think. When a snake yawns, it's not because he's sleepy. Instead, yawning usually has two main functions.

SMELL

Recently, it has been discovered that yawning is an extra way that snakes are able to smell. Similar to tongue flicking, yawning utilizes the Jacobson's organ. When the snake stretches its mouth open wide, scent particles travel directly into the Jacobson's organ. This organ, located on the roof of their mouths, helps their brains process and identify smells.

MEAL PREPARATION

Yawning also helps a snake prepare for large meals. When a snake yawns, he is stretching out his mouth. This helps to expand things to make enough room to engulf large meals.

SNAKES

MUSKING

You probably already knew that some snakes have powerful venom. But did you also know that snakes have stinky, smelly secretions similar to skunks? Eww! Snakes release a nasty, foul-smelling liquid as a warning to predators. This is called musking.

Musking allows snakes to keep predators away without fighting or biting. Predators are anything that the snake perceives as a risk, including large birds, coyotes, or you, so watch out! Musk sends the message to predators that "I will taste gross, so stay away." And guess what: it usually works! All snakes are capable of musking, but some species musk more than others. This is especially true for younger snakes or smaller snakes.

All snakes have what's called a cloacal chamber or vent. It's located near the end of their tails. Musk alone is usually an off-white color and can be somewhat greasy, which makes it especially difficult to wash off. Oftentimes, though, when a snake musks, urine and feces will also be sprayed in combination with the musk. Double yuck! That happens because the cloacal is the same opening that all digestive waste passes through.

Musk smells very different depending on the species of snake. Some snakes spray an odor similar to rotten eggs, others like a skunk, and some just like dead fish. But regardless, the smell is very hard to get rid of!

MOLTING OR SHEDDING

Did you know that snakes are the only animals able to shed their entire skin all at once? This is because when a snake grows, his skin does not. He needs a bigger size, and therefore he sheds his old skin in one piece. He also sheds because his old skin may be getting old or worn out. This process of shedding is called *ecdysis*.

Snakes will typically shed their skin three to four times a year, but that number can vary. Younger snakes that are still growing in size may shed more frequently as they continue to get larger. Some species also tend to shed more frequently than others. Other factors, such as environment and health, will factor into how often a snake sheds.

Tip

If you're curious to know when a snake may soon shed, here are a few signs to look for. Before a snake sheds his skin, his eyes will turn a cloudy bluish color and his skin will look dull. He may also hide more or become more hissy and aggressive or refuse to be held. Some snakes even lose some of their appetite during this time.

SNAKES

77

RELAXED BEHAVIOR

It's important to be able to identify when a snake is relaxed enough to be held or handled. A comfortable, relaxed snake will usually lie in her terrarium not doing much of anything. She might be in her favorite hiding spot or resting on a branch. If the snake is agitated and active, it's probably not the best time to hold her.

CURIOUS BEHAVIOR

A curious snake might also be relaxed, but you will notice her slithering around her enclosure more. She tends to do this during nighttime hours or anytime she is looking for food. You will also notice an increase in tongue flicking as she smells the area for something of possible interest.

SNAKES

STRESSED BEHAVIOR

A stressed snake is fearful and worried. His body will physically look tense and tight. He may also become hyper and quickly dart from one hiding spot to another in an effort to get away. You might also notice that he's more likely to track movement with his eyes or head. Some breeds of snakes will roll into balls when stressed, while others will push away or against you as if to say, "Stay back." Always listen to these cues to avoid an angry snake that may strike.

Fish

80

ERRATIC SWIMMING

It's not uncommon for fish to spontaneously dart and swim across and around the tank. But you should take notice if this behavior becomes a pattern or if it continues for any extended amount of time. That could be a sign that the fish is in distress. Erratic swimming includes behaviors like swimming very fast, darting, swimming in circles or a corkscrew motion, or swimming sideways.

If the fish is showing these behaviors, always begin first by testing the water for quality issues. If the water is unbalanced, it could cause serious health issues that could lead to death if not treated quickly.

FIN NIPPING

Fin nipping is when fish will nip or bite at the fins or tails of other fish. Fin nipping is serious, as it can lead to fin rot and even death in your fish. How do you stop this behavior before it causes too much harm?

Before choosing the fish species that you'll be bringing home to your tank, study up on their qualities. Some species, like serpae tetras and cherry barbs (pictured here), will nip less when in schools of the same species.

You should also avoid placing species known for nipping with any long-finned species. This puts an irresistible target on the long-finned species, saying, "Come bite me!"

FISH

GLASS SURFING

Glass surfing, also called pacing, is when a fish constantly swims back and forth along the glass walls of the aquarium. If you've ever found yourself nervously walking the floor, you've been doing the same thing!

Glass surfing is a sign of a stressed fish. Unfortunately, stress is one of the top causes of death in fish, so this is an important sign to look for.

If your fish is glass surfing, first check the water quality and temperature of the tank. Then look at other environmental clues to determine why your fish may be stressed. Is the tank overstocked with too many fish or overcrowded with decorations? Fish need plenty of room to swim, and just like any other animal, they do not like feeling confined in a small space.

While it's important not to overcrowd the fish tank, it's also necessary to understand what type of natural tendencies your breed(s) of fish have. Some species of fish prefer to live in schools (groups of fish), and being alone can cause stress. They might just need some friends! Other times, you might have a mean fish in the tank that is picking on another fish. A fish that is bullied is likely to glass surf and feel stressed. If this is the case, it's best to separate the fish if possible.

HIDING

Some fish hide simply because they're sleeping. It might seem odd to see that during the daytime, but did you know that some species of fish are nocturnal? Take, for example, the clown pleco or the black ghost knifefish, who will sleep during the day and become active at night.

But if your fish isn't the nocturnal type and hiding is a recent pattern, it may indicate other potential issues like too strong of a current from a filter, the presence of an aggressive fish, or overcrowding. Always examine all aspects of the aquarium and ensure water quality and temperature as well.

SCHOOLS

There are a few aquarium species, like tetras and rainbow fish, that are true schooling fish. Schooling fish usually group very closely together and often swim in the same direction with synchronized movements. These species thrive best in numbers of six or more of their own kind, but if your tank has enough space, the more the better!

85

GASPING FOR AIR

If you ever see a fish swimming to the surface of the water and gasping for air, you know there is an immediate problem. Besides a few species that eat at the surface, this is usually a signal that there are low oxygen levels in the aquarium.

When oxygen is low, fish may at first swim slower or have a decreased appetite. As oxygen levels worsen, you may notice rapid gill movement and then eventually gasping for oxygen at the surface of the water.

Overcrowding is almost always the root cause. This problem can be fixed by increasing your aquarium size or removing large decorations. You should also clean the water regularly and ensure the proper water temperature for your species. If your fish need warmer water, remember that warmer water is not able to hold as much oxygen as cooler water. Aerators or other filters can be added to help.

FISH AGGRESSION

Unfortunately, not all fish get along. If you notice fish fighting, they're probably not going to be good tank mates. If you do have aggressive fish, it is best to separate them with a divider or rehome them. Some fish become so aggressive that they can end up badly hurting or even killing other fish. This can be very sad and frustrating.

Before purchasing any fish, research each species to learn more about their levels of aggression. It's also important to know what other species they are most compatible to live with. If possible, try to have a mix of bottom and top feeders to keep the aquarium balanced. Remember, your aquarium needs to have plenty of space for all of your fish to swim. If living quarters become too small, stress and aggression will increase in your tank.

FISH

DIGGING

Have you ever seen a fish digging in the rocks or other substrate in an aquarium? (Substrate is any material at the bottom of a tank.) Despite what you may be hoping for, no, it's not looking for buried pirate's treasure. But there are a few simple reasons that explain this funny and entertaining behavior.

HIDING

Yes, you guessed it! Some species of fish have shyer personalities and spend more of their time hiding out in the substrate. You may even notice a den or burrow being built out of debris the fish finds in the aquarium. Other diggers make a hole to sleep in or for protection from an aggressive fish.

FEEDING

Fish like catfish and carp will also dig in the sand looking for their food. What look like whiskers are really called barbels. These barbels help them sense food as they dig.

SPAWNING

The last main reason that fish dig is because they are spawning. Spawning is when a fish releases her eggs. Some fish, depending on the species, will dig a hole in the substrate to make a small spawning pit. This pit becomes the perfect nesting spot to store her eggs until hatching time.

FISH

RAPID GILL MOVEMENT

Rapid gill movement is when the breathing rate of a fish increases. This means he begins breathing quicker than normal. Rapid gill movement is usually a sign of a stressed fish.

Some things that could cause stress to a fish include poor water quality and temperature. Test your water frequently for high ammonia, nitrate, nitrite, and pH levels. If the water is not tended regularly, it can become toxic to fish.

Other possible issues that lead to rapid gill movement include an aggressive fish mate or being transported to a new aquarium. In worst-case scenarios, it could even be parasites or diseases like flukes, mikes, or ich. Never ignore any changes in behavior patterns with fish.

LACK OF ENERGY

Being lethargic means having little to no energy. Most fish species swim in the middle of the tank, but a lethargic fish will slow down and spend more time at the bottom or sides of the aquarium. If you notice this sudden behavior in one or more fish, it's usually a sign of stress or sickness. Always check the water quality and temperature first, as that is the most common culprit.

FISH

ABOUT BUSHEL & PECK BOOKS

Bushel & Peck Books is a children's publishing house with a special mission. Through our Book-for-Book Promise™, we donate one book to kids in need for every book we sell. Our beautiful books are given to kids through schools, libraries, local neighborhoods, shelters, nonprofits, and also to many selfless organizations that are working hard to make a difference. So thank you for purchasing this book! Because of you, another book will make its way into the hands of a child who needs it most.

NOMINATE A SCHOOL OR ORGANIZATION TO RECEIVE FREE BOOKS

Do you know a school, library, or organization that could use some free books for their kids? We'd love to help! Please fill out the nomination form on our website, and we'll do everything we can to make something happen.

www.bushelandpeckbooks.com/pages/
nominate-a-school-or-organization

If you liked this book, please leave a review online at your favorite retailer. Honest reviews spread the word about Bushel & Peck—and help us make better books, too!